B+T 9
95
$17.

BUTTERFLIES

BY MARTIN SCHWABACHER

BENCHMARK **B**OOKS

MARSHALL CAVENDISH
NEW YORK

Series Consultant

James G. Doherty

General Curator, Bronx Zoo, New York

Thanks to Dr. Karen Sime of the University of California for her expert reading of this manuscript.

Benchmark Books

Marshall Cavendish

99 White Plains Road

Tarrytown, NY 10591-9001

www.marshallcavendish.com

Library of Congress Cataloging-in-Publication Data

Schwabacher, Martin.

Butterflies / by Martin Schwabacher.

v. cm. – (Animals, animals)

Includes bibliographical references and index.

Contents: Beautiful butterflies – The butterfly family – The big change – Butterfly enemies – Butterflies and people.

ISBN 0-7614-1618-8

1. Butterflies—Juvenile literature. [1. Butterflies. 2. Endangered species.] I. Title. II. Series.

QL544.2.S39 2003

595.78'9–dc21

2003003627

Photo Research by Anne Burns Images

Cover Photo by Animals Animals/Robert Maier

All the photographs used in this book are with permission and through the courtesy of:
Animals Animals: K.Sandved, 6; Michael Fogden, 10; Patti Murray, 15 (bottom right); George Bernard, 28; Breck P.Kent, 30; Fabio Colombini, 31; Doug Wechsler, 32. *Corbis:* Anthony Bannister/ Gallo Images, 18; *Peter Arnold:* Kevin Schafer, 17 (top). George McCarthy, 36. *Visuals Unlimited:* Rob and Ann Simpson, 4; Rick and Nora Bowers, 7; Kjell B.Sandved, 12, 14 (right), 15 (top right); Brian Rogers, 14 (top left); Gary Mezzaros, 14 (bottom left); Leroy Simon, 15 (left); A.Kerstitch, 17 (bottom); Mary Cummins, 20; Bob Wilson, 21; Gustav W. Verderlur, 22, 23; Ray Coleman, 24; Greg VandeLeest, 26; Robert Clay, 34; Tom Edwards, 37.

Printed in China

1 3 5 6 4 2

On the cover: A swallowtail butterfly

CONTENTS

1
BEAUTIFUL BUTTERFLIES

Everyone loves butterflies. Fluttering gently by, butterflies bring a burst of color. No other insect is studied, collected, or just plain enjoyed by so many people.

Did you ever wonder why butterflies never seem to fly in a straight line? It looks as if they are not quite sure where they are going or just are not in much of a hurry. But their wobbly flight serves a purpose. It makes them much harder to catch. A hungry bird cannot swoop down and snatch a butterfly for lunch if it cannot tell which way the butterfly will wobble next.

There are thousands of different *species*, or kinds, of butterflies. Each species has a different pattern of colors on its big, floppy wings. The colors and patterns on butterfly wings are made by thousands of tiny *scales*. These scales give butterflies their scientific name. The group of insects that butterflies and moths belong to is called Lepidoptera, which means scaly winged.

THROUGHOUT HISTORY, BUTTERFLIES HAVE BEEN ADMIRED FOR THEIR DELICATE BEAUTY. THE MALAY LACEWING BUTTERFLY CAN BE FOUND IN THE FORESTS OF MALAYSIA.

If you touch a butterfly wing, you may notice some brightly colored dust on your fingers. This powder is actually the tiny scales that give butterfly wings their color. These scales come off when you touch them because they are attached very loosely. When some moths get caught in sticky spider webs, they can escape and leave behind nothing but some of their loose scales.

Some butterfly wings are dull brown, but others shine like gold and jewels. The brightest scales are partly clear, so when sunlight enters them they glow like pearls or opals.

OWL BUTTERFLIES GET THEIR NAME FROM THE EYESPOTS ON THEIR UNDER-
SIDES THAT LOOK LIKE THE EYES OF AN OWL.

Some scales have many thin layers and shimmer like oil on water. And other scales reflect light in a way that makes them look like shiny metal.

The scales form patterns on a butterfly's wings that tell what type of butterfly it is. These patterns help butterflies to recognize their own species and to hide from *predators*. Some butterfly wings look like leaves, flowers, or tree bark. If the butterfly holds very still while sitting on certain plants it will blend in. This keeps it safe from the many animals that eat butterflies. Other butterflies have large spots on their wings that look like big eyes. These eyespots make the butterfly look like the face of a much larger animal, scaring away predators.

Except for its dazzling wings, a butterfly's body is much like that of any other insect. All insects have three main parts. The head has the mouth, the eyes, and two long stalks called *antennae*, which butterflies use for smelling. The

MANY FLOWERS CANNOT MAKE SEEDS UNLESS A PART OF THE FLOWER CALLED *POLLEN* IS CARRIED TO ANOTHER PLANT. WHEN BUTTERFLIES, BEES, AND OTHER INSECTS FEED ON FLOWERS, POLLEN STICKS TO THEIR BODIES. WHEN THE INSECTS MOVE TO ANOTHER PLANT, THE POLLEN FALLS OFF, HELPING THE PLANT CREATE SEEDS. IN THIS WAY, BOTH PLANT AND INSECT BENEFIT.

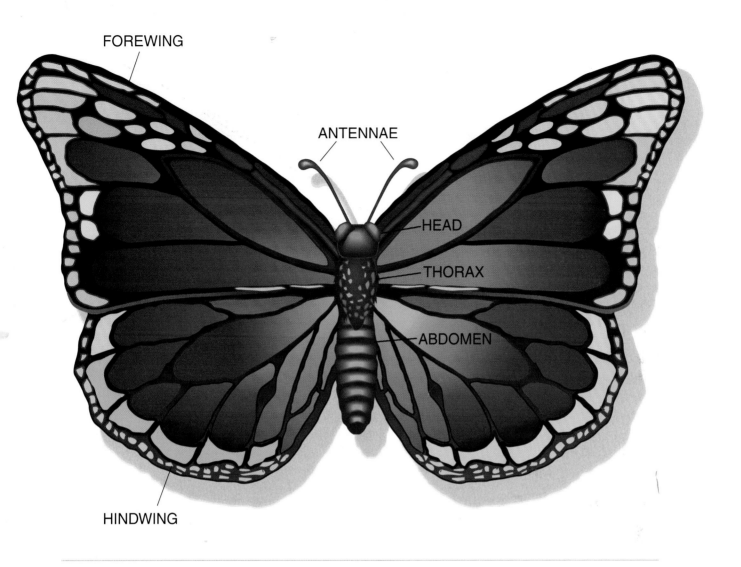

FOREWING

ANTENNAE

HEAD

THORAX

ABDOMEN

HINDWING

middle section, or *thorax*, has everything needed for get–ting around: legs, wings, and strong muscles to move them. Butterflies, like all insects, have six legs. They also have four wings–two on each side. The rear section, or *abdomen*, is used for digesting food, mating, and laying eggs.

ADULT BUTTERFLIES DRINK THROUGH THE PROBOSCIS. WHEN NOT IN USE, THE PROBOSCIS COILS UP.

Adult butterflies eat through a long tube called a *proboscis,* which they use like a drinking straw. Many flowers have sweet liquid called nectar inside. The butterfly sticks its proboscis into the flower and sucks out the nectar.

2
THE BUTTERFLY FAMILY

Butterflies come in an amazing variety of shapes, sizes, and colors. Some can fly thousands of miles while others cannot fly at all. The largest butterflies, called birdwings, have a wingspan of about twelve inches (30 cm). The smallest, called pygmy blues, are less than an inch (1 cm) across.

Butterflies are found almost everywhere in the world. They live on every continent except Antarctica. They live in forests, fields, and on cold mountaintops. Others live in hot deserts, wet rain forests, and even in the icy Arctic.

There are over 150,000 different species of butterflies and moths. But there are many more kinds of moths than butterflies. Only about one out of every ten species in this group is a butterfly. Most of the rest are moths.

A third group called skippers is very closely related to butterflies. Some people consider them a kind of butterfly. Like butterflies, skippers are brightly colored and fly during the day, but their antennae are hooked and they hold their wings at a different angle.

SWALLOWTAIL BUTTERFLIES GET THEIR NAME FROM THE LONG "TAILS" ON THEIR HINDWINGS THAT LOOK A BIT LIKE THE LONG, POINTED TAILS OF SWALLOWS (A TYPE OF BIRD).

BUTTERFLY SPECIES
HERE ARE JUST A FEW OF THE THOUSANDS OF BUTTERFLY SPECIES.

BIRDWING
This is the largest butterfly with a wingspan that can reach 12 inches (30 cm) across.

BLUE MORPHO
The blue shimmering wings are brown with bronze eyespots underneath.

APOLLO
These are found in mountainous regions.

JULIA

The bright wing color of this tropical butterfly warns predators that they are poisonous.

GLASSWING

Partially transparent wings make these butterflies difficult for predators to find.

PYGMY BLUE

This is the smallest butterfly with a wingspan less than an inch (2.5 cm) across.

WHAT IS THE DIFFERENCE BETWEEN A BUTTERFLY AND A MOTH?

There are no hard and fast rules, but here are some clues:

- Butterflies tend to be brightly colored, while most moths are dull brown or whitish.
- If it is flying during the day, it is probably a butterfly. Most moths only come out at night.
- Butterflies have long, thin antennae with a club on the end. Moths lack these clubs, and male moths often have antennae that look like wide feathers.
- Most butterflies hold their wings straight up or straight out when they are resting. Moths usually have their wings tucked flat behind their bodies.

None of these rules is true for every species. For instance, some moths have brilliant colors, while some butterflies are dull-colored.

A MOTH (ABOVE) FOLDS ITS WINGS OVER ITS BACK WHILE RESTING. A BUTTERFLY AT REST (LEFT) HOLDS ITS WINGS EITHER STRAIGHT OUT OR STRAIGHT UP.

3
THE BIG CHANGE

Butterflies change shape three times in their lives. First they change from an egg into a caterpillar, or *larva*. Then they become a *chrysalis*, which at last turns into a butterfly. At each stage, they have a very different job to do.

A female butterfly lays between one hundred and 1,000 eggs. She looks for the kind of leaves her offspring will eat and lays her eggs right on them, often glued to the underside.

When a butterfly egg hatches, a caterpillar crawls out. It has no wings and looks like a worm on legs. Though adult butterflies have six legs, caterpillars have sixteen— six true legs and ten stubby legs called *prolegs*.

Most caterpillars eat only one type of plant. Some will eat only a certain part of a certain kind of plant, and nothing else. But others eat many different kinds of plants.

Caterpillars shed their skin and head coverings several times as they grow. The main job of a caterpillar is to eat and grow. They have powerful jaws for chewing leaves.

CATERPILLARS BEGIN EATING AS SOON AS THEY COME OUT OF THEIR EGGS. THEIR FIRST MEAL IS USUALLY THEIR OWN EGGSHELL.

MOST BUTTERFLIES LAY THEIR EGGS ON THE UNDERSIDE OF LEAVES. THAT WAY, THE BABY CATERPILLARS CAN EAT THE PLANT AS SOON AS THEY HATCH.

Most eat almost without stopping and become hundreds of times larger than when they first came out of their eggs.

Some species remain caterpillars for just a couple of weeks, while others stay in this stage for up to two years. But at some point, all caterpillars stop eating and turn into a *pupa* or chrysalis. In this stage, they begin their change, or *metamorphosis*, from a caterpillar to an adult butterfly. Many moths cover their bodies with silk, making a case called a cocoon. But most butterflies do not make cocoons. Instead, they grow a hard shell around their bodies and

20

CATERPILLAR'S HAVE SIX TRUE LEGS AND TEN PROLEGS.

hang from a bit of silk. These butterfly pupae often look shiny, as if they were made of metal.

The pupa hangs completely still, but inside, the butter–fly's body is being taken apart and put back together. For some butterflies, this takes just two weeks. Other species

A PUPA SHELL IS SOFT AT FIRST, BUT QUICKLY BECOMES A HARD, PROTECTIVE CASE.

remain a pupa for over a year. When the adult butterfly is fully grown, it tears a hole in its covering and climbs out. It is wet and limp, and its wings are soft and crumpled. Then the wings unfold and fill up like an air mattress. After an hour or more, the wings become stiff. Only then can the butterfly fly.

As a caterpillar, the butterfly's job was to eat and grow. Now, as an adult, its main goal is to mate and lay eggs.

THE MONARCH BUTTERFLY INSIDE THIS LATE-STAGE PUPA IS NEARLY READY TO COME OUT.

Butterflies do not need to eat as much as caterpillars, because they have finished growing. Some adult moths never eat. They just mate, lay eggs, and die. But most must eat to get energy to fly.

When it is time to mate, male and female butterflies find each other partly by smell. The female gives off odors that the male smells with his antennae. Males also give off odors that make females want to mate with them. The

IT WILL TAKE ABOUT AN HOUR FOR THIS NEWLY EMERGED BUTTERFLY TO GET READY TO FLY.

colors and patterns on their wings also help them find each other. Some species mate while flying. After mating, the female lays eggs that will grow into new butterflies, starting the whole cycle over again.

In places with long, cold winters or very hot summers, it may take two years for a single batch of eggs to grow to adulthood. When there is no food, butterflies might spend a long time resting and waiting, as eggs, caterpillars, pupas, or adults. When the weather improves, they come out to eat. In places where the weather is always warm, the complete cycle from egg to adult occurs continually throughout the year.

4
BUTTERFLY ENEMIES

It might not seem like one little butterfly or caterpillar could eat very much. But there are millions and millions of caterpillars in the world. A large group of them can strip all the leaves off one tree or an entire forest. Put together, caterpillars eat more total plants than any other kind of animal.

By eating plants, caterpillars create useful food for other animals. Many animals cannot eat leaves–but they can eat caterpillars. Millions of butterflies and caterpillars are eaten by other animals every day. Leaves have very little protein, but caterpillars' bodies are full of protein. Spiders, beetles, frogs, lizards, birds, bats, wasps, and mice all eat caterpillars or adult butterflies. These animals then become food for larger animals.

Since so many animals want to eat them, caterpillars and butterflies need some way to defend themselves. This is not easy, because they do not have a hard shell or any

A LEAFWING BUTTERFLY IS ALMOST IMPOSSIBLE TO SEE WHEN RESTING ON A BRANCH.

SOME CATERPILLARS ARE SO SMALL THEY BURROW INSIDE A LEAF AND EAT IT FROM WITHIN.

way to fight back. And though butterflies can often fly away, caterpillars are very slow moving. To other animals, a caterpillar's soft, plump body is hard to resist. Though caterpillars get eaten by the millions every day, others survive by using a few tricks to avoid predators.

One way to keep from being eaten is to avoid being seen. Some caterpillars look just like the plants they feed on. Some look just like green leaves while others look like twigs. Some are oddly shaped so they look like the jagged edge of a leaf, or a dried, curled-up dead leaf. And some attach leaf parts or twig pieces to their bodies, making them even harder to see.

Even better than blending into the background is to stay out of sight completely. Many caterpillars make nests by rolling or folding up a leaf and hiding inside. Some build a large tent of silk. Others dig small tunnels into wood or underground. Some make a little bag or case of silk and leaves that they carry around with them to hide in.

Some caterpillars, however, stay boldly in the open. Instead of blending in with the background, they are very brightly colored. Many of these are protected by bushy hairs, which make them unpleasant to swallow. In some caterpillars, these spiny hairs are hollow and contain poison.

VICEROY BUTTERFLIES (ABOVE) MIMIC THE COLORING OF POISONOUS MONARCHS (RIGHT) SO PREDATORS WILL STAY AWAY.

These hairs can stick into attackers and cause pain or sicken them. Some moth larvae spit or vomit foul-smelling juices onto attackers.

Many caterpillars and adult butterflies defend themselves with poison in another way. They eat poisonous plants that fill their bodies with poison but do not harm them. If a bird eats the caterpillar or butterfly, it gets sick

30

from the poison—and makes sure never to eat that kind of butterfly again.

The pattern on a poisonous butterfly's wings is a warning to stay away. Some butterflies that are not poisonous look just like these poisonous butterflies. Animals will not eat insects that they think may be poisonous, so these imposters are safe.

CAN YOU FIND THE CLACKER BUTTERFLY IN THIS PICTURE?

Some butterflies have wing patterns that look like large eyes, called eyespots. Seeing these eyespots may make a predator think it is looking at a much larger animal. Some wings are dull on one side and bright on the other. When a bird spots such a butterfly, it might see the bright side of the wing flash and then disappear. This confuses the bird. All these tricks help to keep butterflies out of harm's way.

5

PEOPLE AND BUTTERFLIES

While butterflies are among the world's best-loved small creatures, they can also cause severe problems. Caterpillars eat important crops such as grains, fruits, sugarcane, cotton, and wood. Moths sometimes get into people's closets and eat wool clothes, silk, furs, and even feathers.

But on the whole, the world would be much worse off without butterflies. Many animals depend on butterflies for food. Some people eat butterflies too. In Africa, the larvae of some skippers are collected and eaten. In Mexico, giant skipper larvae are so popular they are canned and sold as treats.

Because many butterflies can only eat a certain kind of plant or live in a certain place, they can be in great danger when people change the land where a particular species lives. One beautiful butterfly, the Xerces blue, became *extinct* when the city of San Francisco, California grew larger

MANY NATURAL HISTORY MUSEUMS AND BOTANICAL GARDENS HAVE BUTTERFLY EXHIBITS AND GARDENS.

LARGE COPPER BUTTERFLIES BECAME EXTINCT IN BRITAIN. SCIENTISTS THEN BROUGHT GROUPS OF THESE BUTTERFLIES FROM EUROPE AND REESTABLISHED THEM IN BRITAIN.

and took away its living space. The large copper butterfly became extinct when people drained the swampy land where it lived in England.

The most beautiful butterflies are also *endangered* because people collect them. In New Guinea, it is illegal to collect giant birdwing butterflies. Without laws like this to protect them, they could disappear forever. Today, some beautiful butterflies are raised on butterfly farms so they

MANY TYPES OF FLOWERS ATTRACT BUTTERFLIES. SOME BUTTERFLY GARDENS, LIKE THIS ONE, INCLUDE A BUTTERFLY HOUSE WHERE BUTTERFLIES CAN FIND SHELTER DURING BAD WEATHER.

can be sold to collectors, thus decreasing the threat to those species in the wild.

One butterfly at special risk is the monarch. Millions of monarchs fly from all over the United States to spend the winter in Mexico. Entire trees can be covered, bending from their weight. But the forests where they spend the winter are being cut down because the people who live there need wood for firewood and land for farming.

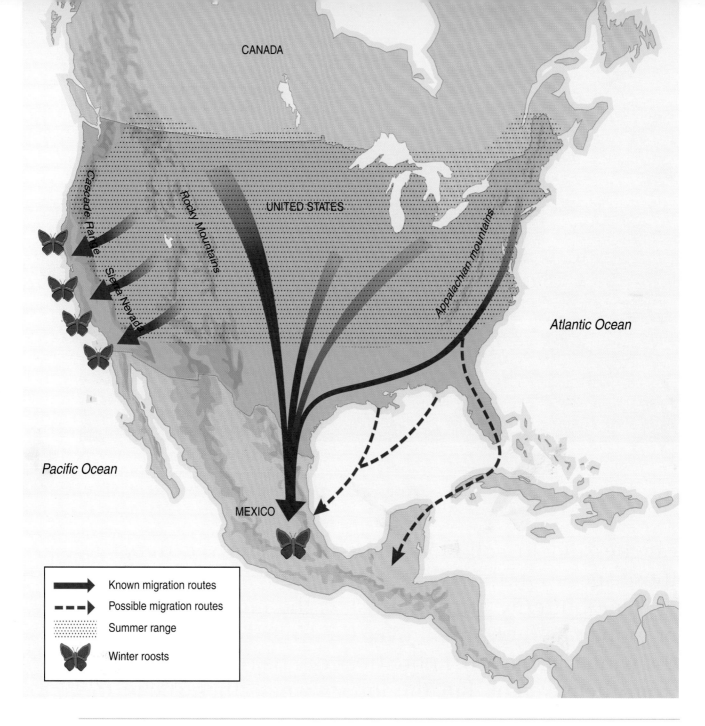

THIS MAP SHOWS THE FALL MIGRATION ROUTES OF MONARCH BUTTERFLIES.

38

People have tried to come up with ways to help both the farmers and the butterflies. Instead of cooking over open fires, some farmers now use special stoves that use much less wood. They also build houses of *adobe*. These houses last longer than wooden houses, and fewer trees are cut to make them. Butterfly lovers hope ideas like these will save the monarchs from becoming extinct.

abdomen: The rear section of an insect's body, which is used for digesting food and laying eggs.

adobe: Clay or mud that is mixed with straw to make bricks.

antennae: A pair of long, narrow, flexible feelers on an insect's head.

chrysalis: The pupa of a butterfly.

endangered: Threatened or placed in danger of harm or extinction.

extinct: Gone forever.

larva: The young, wormlike stage of an insect's life before it has wings.

metamorphosis: A complete change in shape and structure, as when a larva changes to an adult insect.

pollen: A fine powder produced by plants that is needed to make seeds.

predators: Animals that hunt other animals.

proboscis: A long, flexible tube on an insect's head used to suck liquid food into the mouth.

prolegs: Stubby legs found on a caterpillar, but not on an adult butterfly.

pupa: The stage in an insect's life during which it changes from a larva to an adult.

scales: A tiny, flat plate; large numbers of scales may cover an animal's body.

species: A single kind of animal or plant.

thorax: The middle section of an insect's body, to which the legs and wings are attached.

BOOKS

Feltwell, John. *Eyewitness Explorers: Butterflies and Moths*. New York: Dorling Kindersley, 1997.

Gibbons, Gail. *Monarch Butterfly*. New York: Holiday House, 1991.

Hamilton, Kersten. *The Butterfly Book: A Kid's Guide to Attracting, Raising, and Keeping Butterflies*. Emeryville, CA: Avalon Travel Publishing, 1997.

Opler, Paul A. *Peterson First Guide to Butterflies and Moths*. New York: Houghton Mifflin, 1998.

Rosenblatt, Lynn. *Monarch Magic! Butterfly Activities and Nature Discoveries*. Madison, WI: Turtleback Books, 1998.

Stokes, Donald, Justin L. Brown and Lillian Q. Stokes. *Stokes Beginner's Guide to Butterflies*. Boston: Little Brown, 2001.

Whalley, Paul. *Butterfly and Moth: Eyewitness Books*. New York: Knopf, 1988.

Wright, Amy Bartlett. *Peterson First Guide to Caterpillars of North America*. New York: Houghton Mifflin, 1998.

VIDEOS

Butterflies for Beginners. Audubon Society. Mastervision, 1996.

How to Attract Mason Bees, Butterflies, and Hummingbirds. Ed Hume. Education 2000, 1994.

The Magic Schoolbus: Butterflies. A Vision, 1999.

WEB SITES

Butterflies of North America: Checklists and photos of butterflies in every U.S. state.

www.npwrc.usgs.gov/resource/distr/lepid/bflyusa/bflyusa.htm

Butterfly Basics: Web site of the Field Museum of Natural History

www.fmnh.org.butterfly/default.htm

The Butterfly Farm: Fast facts and photos.

www.butterflyfarm.co.cr/

Butterfly Migration Game

www.twingroves.district96.k12.il.us/Wetlands/WetlandGames/
    Monarch/MonarchGame.html

Children's Butterfly Site: Coloring pages, facts, and links

www.mesc.usgs.gov/resources/education/butterfly/bfly_intro.asp

Monarch Watch: Advice on growing a butterfly garden

www.monarchwatch.org/

ABOUT THE AUTHOR

Martin Schwabacher is the author of more than twenty books for young people, including *Elephants*, *Bears*, and *Frogs* in the Animals Animals series. He is also a writer for the American Museum of Natural History, where he has contributed to the Museum's permanent halls, exhibitions, online courses, and Web sites. He lives in New York City with his wife Melissa McDaniel, a children's book writer and editor, and their daughter Iris.

INDEX

Page numbers for illustrations are in **boldface.**